Cool Cars

BUGATTI

BY DALTON RAINS

WWW.APEXEDITIONS.COM

Copyright © 2026 by Apex Editions, Mendota Heights, MN 55120. All rights reserved. No part of this book may be reproduced or utilized in any form or by any means without written permission from the publisher.

Apex is distributed by North Star Editions:
sales@northstareditions.com | 888-417-0195

Produced for Apex by Red Line Editorial.

Photographs ©: GDA/El Universal/Mexico/AP Images, cover; Shutterstock Images, 1, 4–5, 14–15, 16–17, 18, 19, 20, 21, 25, 26–27, 29; Hans Blossey/imageBROKER.com GmbH & Co. KG/Alamy, 6; Martyn Lucy/Getty Images News/Getty Images, 8–9; National Motor Museum/Heritage Images/Hulton Archive/Getty Images, 10–11; Bruno De Hogues/Sygma/Getty Images, 12; Richard Bord/Getty Images News/Getty Images, 13; Nicolas Genin/Abaca/Sipa USA/AP Images, 22–23; Martyn Lucy/Getty Images Sport/Getty Images, 24

Library of Congress Control Number: 2024952631

ISBN
979-8-89250-519-2 (hardcover)
979-8-89250-555-0 (paperback)
979-8-89250-626-7 (ebook pdf)
979-8-89250-591-8 (hosted ebook)

Printed in the United States of America
Mankato, MN
082025

NOTE TO PARENTS AND EDUCATORS

Apex books are designed to build literacy skills in striving readers. Exciting, high-interest content attracts and holds readers' attention. The text is carefully leveled to allow students to achieve success quickly. Additional features, such as bolded glossary words for difficult terms, help build comprehension.

TABLE OF CONTENTS

CHAPTER 1
SUPER SPEED 4

CHAPTER 2
HISTORY 10

CHAPTER 3
VEYRONS AND CHIRONS 16

CHAPTER 4
RARE MODELS 22

COMPREHENSION QUESTIONS • 28
GLOSSARY • 30
TO LEARN MORE • 31
ABOUT THE AUTHOR • 31
INDEX • 32

CHAPTER 1

SUPER SPEED

A **supercar** zooms around a test track. It's a Bugatti Chiron Super Sport. The driver veers around a bend. The Bugatti makes the turn with ease.

The Bugatti Chiron Super Sport came out in 2019.

The Bugatti reaches a long straightaway. Its engine rumbles. The car goes faster and faster.

FAST FACT

The Super Sport used a track in Germany. The track is one of the only places supercars can reach top speeds.

◀ **The Super Sport sped around a test track. One stretch is flat and straight for 5.4 miles (8.7 km).**

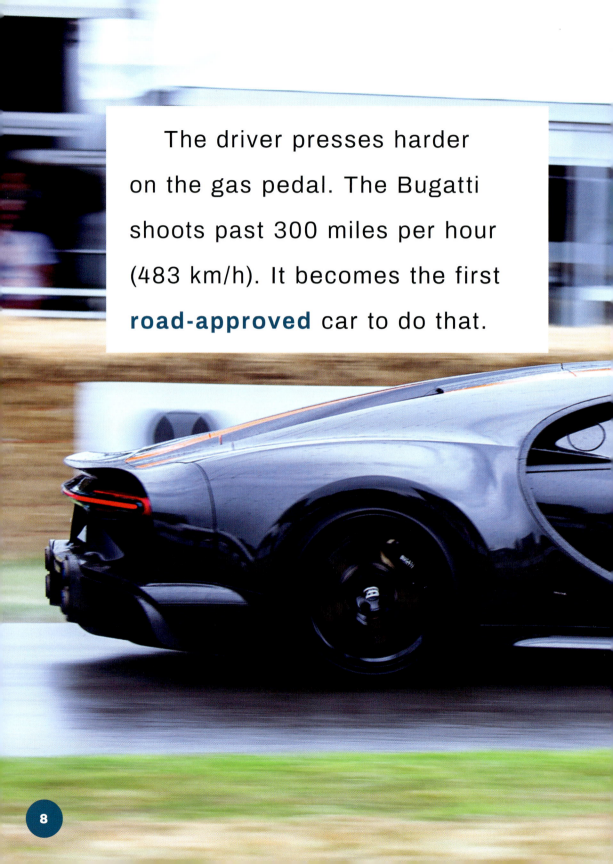

The driver presses harder on the gas pedal. The Bugatti shoots past 300 miles per hour (483 km/h). It becomes the first **road-approved** car to do that.

AIRFLOW

Aerodynamics help supercars reach high speeds. Air must flow smoothly around a car's front. Otherwise, the car can shake and lose control. Air must also push down the back. That keeps the tires on the ground.

The Bugatti Chiron Super Sport reached a top speed of 304.773 miles per hour (490.485 km/h).

CHAPTER 2

History

Ettore Bugatti began building cars in the 1900s. He started his company in 1909. Bugatti's race cars became very successful. The Type 35 won more than 2,500 races.

Ettore Bugatti stands next to a Type 35. This car was made between 1924 and 1931.

There were only six Type 41 Royales ever built.

Bugatti also made **luxury** cars. He built the first Type 41 Royale in 1926. This long car featured a massive engine. It also had a smooth, curving look.

FIRST OF ITS KIND

Bugatti built the Type 57SC Atlantic in the 1930s. Its body had a teardrop shape. Only four Type 57SCs exist. But their shape **inspired** many future Bugattis.

The teardrop shape of the Type 57SC Atlantic helped its aerodynamics.

In 1956, Bugatti stopped making cars. It went out of business for years. Volkswagen bought the **brand** in 1998. New Bugattis hit the roads.

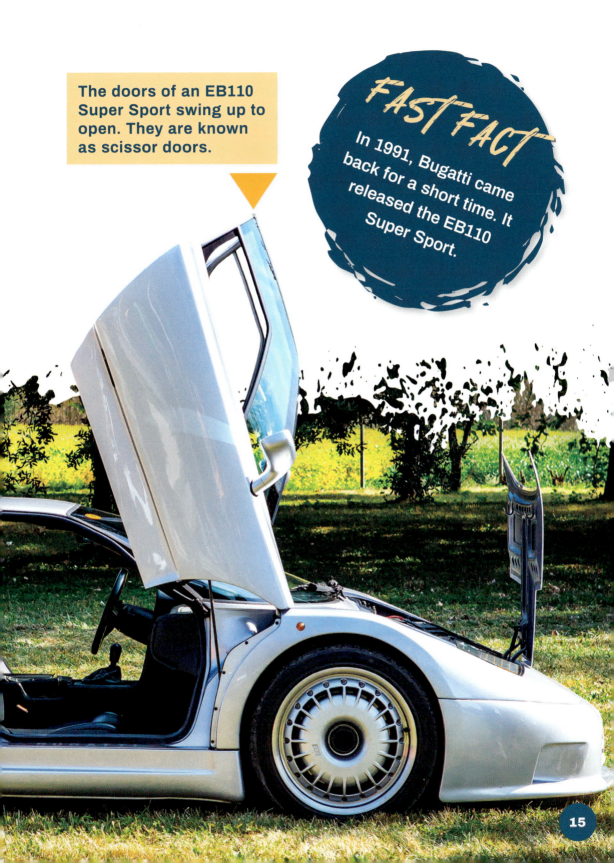

The doors of an EB110 Super Sport swing up to open. They are known as scissor doors.

FAST FACT

In 1991, Bugatti came back for a short time. It released the EB110 Super Sport.

CHAPTER 3

VEYRONS AND CHIRONS

In the late 1990s, **engineers** started on the Veyron. First, they **designed** a powerful engine. Then, they planned an aerodynamic body.

The Bugatti Veyron gets lower to the ground at high speeds. That keeps it from rolling over.

It cost almost $50,000 to replace a Veyron's tires.

The first Veyrons came out in 2005. Almost every part had to be built from scratch. Even the tires were designed for high speeds.

MORE RECORDS

In 2010, a Bugatti Veyron broke a speed record. It reached 267.9 miles per hour (431.1 km/h). That was faster than all other road-approved cars.

The 2010 Veyron Super Sport could hit 60 miles per hour (97 km/h) in less than 2.5 seconds.

Bugatti built 500 Chirons. People paid between $2 million and $4 million for each car.

In 2016, new models replaced Veyrons. Chirons built on the best parts of Veyrons. However, they had some key differences. Chirons had sharper edges. They had better engine cooling, too.

FAST FACT
The Bugatti Tourbillon replaced the Chiron in 2024. It added three electric **motors**.

The Tourbillon was Bugatti's first hybrid car. Hybrid cars run on both gasoline and electricity.

CHAPTER 4

RARE MODELS

Bugatti made several rarer models, too. The Divo was one. It was slower than the Chiron. But the Divo turned much more smoothly.

Only 40 Bugatti Divos were ever made.

Bugatti released the Mistral in 2024.

Drivers could enjoy the wind in the roofless Mistral. This car combined traditional and new styles. Like many older Bugattis, it had a horseshoe-shaped grille.

THE CENTODIECI

Bugatti built only 10 Centodiecis. The cars brought back features from the EB110. Both models had large rear wings. Both also had five air holes on each side.

Like the EB110, the Centodieci has a small curved grille at the front of its hood.

Only one La Voiture Noire exists. It was inspired by the 57SC Atlantic. People waited to see what car Bugatti would make next. It was sure to catch plenty of eyes out on the road.

The only La Voiture Noire sold for nearly $19 million in 2019. It was the most expensive Bugatti at the time.

FAST FACT

La Voiture Noire means "The Black Car" in French.

27

COMPREHENSION
QUESTIONS

Write your answers on a separate piece of paper.

1. Write a few sentences explaining the main ideas of Chapter 3.

2. Which Bugatti model would you most like to drive? Why?

3. When did the first Veyrons come out?
    - A. 2005
    - B. 2010
    - C. 2013

4. What allowed more Bugattis to be built after the company went out of business?
    - A. Bugatti never stopped making cars.
    - B. A Bugatti broke a speed record.
    - C. Volkswagen bought the brand.

5. What does **veers** mean in this book?

*The driver **veers** around a bend. The Bugatti makes the turn with ease.*

    A. continues straight
    B. loses control
    C. changes direction

6. What does **traditional** mean in this book?

*This car combined **traditional** and new styles. Like many older Bugattis, it had a horseshoe-shaped grille.*

    A. unlike anything made before
    B. based on ideas from the past
    C. not known by many people

Answer key on page 32.

GLOSSARY

aerodynamics
The ways that air flows around a solid object.

brand
The products and services connected with one carmaker.

designed
Planned how to make or build something.

engineers
People who use math and science to solve problems.

inspired
Started or gave the idea for something.

luxury
Having to do with things that are high quality, comfortable, and often expensive.

motors
Machines that cause something to move.

road-approved
Able to be driven on public roads, not just test tracks.

supercar
A car fast enough for racing that can also go on the street.

BOOKS

Lowell, Barbara. *Sports Cars*. Black Rabbit Books, 2024.
Rains, Dalton. *Formula 1 Racing*. Apex Editions, 2024.
Sommer, Nathan. *Bugatti Chiron*. Bellwether Media, 2023.

ONLINE RESOURCES

Visit **www.apexeditions.com** to find links and resources related to this title.

ABOUT THE AUTHOR

Dalton Rains is a writer and editor from St. Paul, Minnesota. He would love to drive a Bugatti someday.

INDEX

B
Bugatti, Ettore, 10

C
Centodieci, 25
Chiron, 4, 7–8, 20–21, 22
Chiron Super Sport, 4, 7–8

D
Divo, 22

E
EB110 Super Sport, 15, 25

L
La Voiture Noire, 26–27

M
Mistral, 24

T
Tourbillon, 21
Type 35, 10
Type 41 Royale, 12
Type 57SC Atlantic, 13, 26

V
Veyron, 16, 18–20
Volkswagen, 14

ANSWER KEY:
1. Answers will vary; 2. Answers will vary; 3. A; 4. C; 5. C; 6. B